Organic Chaos

Evana Victoria

BookLeaf Publishing

Presentation by *BookLeaf Publishing*

Web: www.bookleafpub.com

E-mail: info@bookleafpub.com

ISBN: 9789357618229

First edition 2022

To my Nonna and my Soul Sister; without you two, this wouldn't be possible.

My sister, who puts up with my crazy; and my best friend who encourages the crazy.

And my mom, thank you.

PREFACE

There's somethings I wish I could say out loud;
but I'm braver on paper.

Hello?

My ears are ringing
the night is calling.
Listen carefully
for they seldom repeat.
Listen cautiously
because they speak the truth.

My ears are ringing
they're telling me secrets,
and those I cannot share.

Suddenly, it's stopped

We are connected

There's no hiding now.

Phantom

I can feel you lurking in my dreams
showing up in places
I thought you'd never visit.

I can feel you
awakening all these feelings
I swear I had buried.

I can feel you under my skin
letting me know
you never really left.

I can feel you infecting me again
with emotions I forgot about
and of visions of what could be.

I can feel you in my heart
filling it with ideas
that can't fit in with reality.

I can feel you picking away
at the wall around my heart
I built because of you.

I can feel you in my thoughts

engulfing me
with feelings I want so much.

I can feel you
tying us together.

But worst of all...

I can feel the pressure mounting,
it's getting out of control
I can feel it coming to the surface
about to overflow.

I can feel the pressure mounting
and I cannot help but cry out.
You have weaseled your way back into my heart.

And I can hear you whispering

"It is I, who owns your soul."

Stars

I'm going to sleep with my window open
so I can finally see the stars.

I've been locked in the ground for so long,
I actually forgot what they were like.

So I'm going to sleep,
with my eyes upon the stars,
because knowing that they're there
comforts me.

And if the sun awakens me
well...
it's going to be a beautiful sight to behold.

Floating

I see you floating beneath the surface,
will you ever come back to me?

The story is long,
but it never gets old.

We met,
we grew close,
Trouble arose,
I tried to save you.
But you can't fight fate,
destiny that's written in stone.
You fell from my clutches
and into the water below.

So here I wait
by the shore where the waters took you
because our story is not nearly done
you will come back,
and you will come back to me
that, my love, is written in the stars.

I see you floating
getting closer each passing year.

Soon, darling, soon.
You will rise from your watery sleep
and we shall claim what is rightfully yours.

Ocean

The ocean, she calls to me
while I am stranded here on land.
Like a siren she calls,
but I am forbidden to answer.

The ocean is waiting
beaconing me with an openness that cannot be
matched,
promising me peace that my soul yearns,
promising me life that my heart desires.

But I am stuck, stranded, marooned on land
forced to look but not touch
forced to yearn for what will make my mind
still.

The ocean is calling,
calling,
Yet....

It's out of my reach.

Escape

There's an island within sight
that I would like to swim to

An island all to myself
but maybe you'd come too

There's an island out there
and it's calling my name

So take my shoes,
take my phone

I won't need them
where I'm going

I'll come back eventually,
but I won't be the same.

Let's go

Let's set off into the sunset
leave everyone behind.

The liars, the thieves, the fakes.

Let's leave them all behind.

We'll go off into the horizon
travel roads yet paved.

We'll forget about our weaknesses and pretend to
be brave.

I'm setting off into the sunset, leaving my
baggage behind.
I'm off to find a place, where I can finally
unwind.
I'm setting off into the sun, so the dark cannot
find me.

Flicker

The lamp post flickers
but mostly stays off
What used to be my greatest muse
has become the symbol of my thoughts.

Here, strong but quick to fade
Not to return but for a moment or two.

The light that used to light my way
has broken, faded and wasted away.

But sometimes it comes back
burns brilliant
and I'm able to hold my thoughts within my
grasp
Spilling out tears of joy
at a passion I had feared burnt out.

Sadly, much like the lamp post.
The light never stays
and we are plunged into darkness again.

No tomorrow

I wish tomorrow would never come
and that the sky would swallow the sun

I wish that the moon will never set
and the sun to never rise

I wish for a never ending night
because once the sun rises

You will be gone,

Forever

from my sight.

To a land where I cannot follow

So tonight, I wish for no tomorrow.

Box Heart

Box heart has edges
Sharp enough to cut
Corners to hide in
And never leave
Shadows to mask secrets
So one one can ever see
What truly hides inside
Is a secret safe with me
Come inside my box heart
I'll let you in for free
But don't expect to ever leave
Because once you're safely tucked away
I'll never set you free

Said

Do you ever look to the sky
Close your eyes and pray real hard
Do you ever go out at night
Look to the stars and ask them, "why?"
Do you wish...
...I never said goodbye?

Glory

Fuck these nights of vivid dreams,
twisting our hearts and
leaving us shattered as the sun rises.
Damn you!
Damn you and your glory.

For leaving us there,
on the side of the road,
standing in the dust,
betrayed in the worst way.
I curse you.
You and yours...

Unraveled at the seams,
you tear apart my heart,
leaving nothing left.
What you have
is what I dream.
What I dream,
I cannot have.

My glory,
my dream;
will never come true.
Your glory,

is my hell.

I can't help but come back for more.

So once again,
I curse you,
You and your glory.
The very thing you stole from me.

Tyrant

You claim you are holy
But you're a liar
You clam to love us
Yet you stab us in the back
You're supposed to be forgiving
But you'll shame us at the drop of a hat

Beware prodigal son, beware.
When You damn the broken,
Be ready to meet us in hell.

Organic Chaos

I miss this
The laughs
The sun
Stories.

I miss the time.
It used to be every year, then every two. Then
maybe half of us or maybe none.

Times change, people grow, lives drift and then
all of a sudden the world stops and no one
moves. And then within a blink of an eye you
realize the time.

And you think of everything you miss, because
there's nothing else to do.

And you miss everything.

The yelling
The stories
The never ending talking over each other,
dozens of voices all reaching concert levels and
all you can wish is for someone to just stop
talking but also wishing for them to never stop.

And stay.

It's organized chaos
Organic chaos
Energy seeping out of every corner and you
can't help but run from it but also bask because

F I N A L L Y.

sometimes it's days, or months
But usually longer, like 10 years longer.

Ten.

Years.

But they're here. And they're loud. And it's
chaos and some are different, some are new,
others have passed on and others just stay the
same.

How have you not changed!?

And there's groups that go off and chat or
hangout or are drawn to the water and they get
to stay out longer because, it's been ten years,
and it's always the same group that you can't get
out of the water

Seriously, we're hungry, let's go!

And you realize with the distance that the fights from before don't matter. Why were you even mad in the first place? You forgive. You move on. You laugh, you heal

You. Heal.

And before you know it, it's time to say goodbye, but that takes over a hour and you drag it out for as long as you can. Because you don't know when it'll be the next time. You don't know who will be still around.

You don't know.

So you savour. You drag those feet for as long as you can. Tomorrow will still be there, but right now...

You cant rush it.

So, hello. Goodbye. I wish you the best. Come back and stay.

I love you. And I miss you. Forever.

Photos

There a moment to be captured
a moment to cherish
something that happened
that left you gasping for air

There's laughter in the image
joy alive in their eyes
but all you see are stills

A fleeting moment in time.

Alice

"Come find me Alice," I sing
as I dance along in front of you

"Come find me Alice..."

I am the green in the moss
the blue in the sky
the brown of the earth

Come find me Alice,
before it's too late
and I am lost forever
in a state of suspended bliss

Snowflakes

Let's catch snowflakes on our tongues
throw our arms out and spin round and round
and round.
Let's get into the car while it's snowing,
crank the wheel until we are spinning.
Let's do this as one,
with smiles on our faces and laughter in our
lungs.
Let's scream it to the clouds, the moon, the stars,
the gods.
We are here, alive, happy and free.

So come, gather around
and come spin out of control with me.

Birth day

On the day of my birth,
bask me in the moonlight
let it recharge my soul,
replenish my heart,
and give me the strength to carry on.

On the day of my birth
leave me in the moonlight,
in the middle of nowhere
with only the moon and stars as my guide.

On the day of my birth,
leave me with the moon,
leave us in silence
so we may become whole once again.

Frozen

It's summertime where they are
they're running, jumping, celebrating
they're embracing, indulging, experiencing

The sun is out
and it's time to live
the sun is back
from its annuall slumber.

Everyone is out
Alive
loving under the warm summer sun.

There's no more cold, fears or hiding
the biting wind is gone
replaced by a sunny breeze.

They welcome back the warmth
like an old friend with open arms,
a hug to soothe their weary souls.

Summer is a grateful reprieve
from the chilling grips of winter.

Winter brings out the worst,

it tires our souls.

Summer soothes us,
rejuvenates us.

It's summertime where they are...

but

we're still caught in the dead of winter

there's no reprieve for us.

Transcending

You never thought you'd see the day,
where everything is calm
and everything is silent.

The weight in your chest is gone,
the pendulum above your head has vanished.

The darkness is behind you.
You've reached the light,
everything is clear;
It's bliss.

But the darkness is still there,
it's scarred onto your heart.

But, for now, you made it….

You made it to the other side…

And it's breathtaking

Goodbye

In order for you to miss me
I have to leave
even though I hate the thought
I need to pack my bags and move on
My time here has come
and I need to move on
and see places you've never heard of.

So goodbye, goodbye
sweet angel of mine
I shall find you the next time I'm in.

But if fate should have it
and we pass on before we meet again
I shall see you in the other side.

So goodbye, goodbye
to the light of my life
I shall see you,
In our next life.